CW00520821

Cleaning Eating wit Granola

Delicious Combination to Keep You Satisfied

by Chloe Tucker

© 2021 Chloe Tucker All Rights Reserved.

License Notes

All rights reserved. This publication cannot be distributed, reproduced, recorded, photocopied, or transmitted. If you desire to share this content, you must seek prior permission from the author. Beware, the author will not be held responsible for your interpretation of this content. However, it is fair to say that the content written herein is accurate.

Table of Contents

Introduction 5

No-Bake Flaked Coconut Granola Bars 7

Chewy Dry Fruit No-Bake Cookies... 9

No-Bake Fudgy Granola Bars 11

No-Bake Oatmeal and Blueberry Bars 13

No-Bake Chocolate Granola Bars 15

Flaked Coconut Granola Bars 17

Gluten-Free and Oat-Free Granola Bars 19

No-Bake Honey and Oat Peanut Granola Bars 21

Chewy No-Bake Granola Bars.. 23

Granola Bars with Oats.. 25

Honey Peanut Granola.. 27

Snack Time Granola Bars 29

Chocolate Granola Bars 31

Amazing Granola Snacks.. 33

Vegan Coconut-Oat Bars 35

Microwave Granola Bars 37

Nut-Free Granola Bars.. 39

No-Bake Chocolate Oat Bars... 42

Simplest Granola Bars 44

Healthy Nutella Granola Bars 46

Gingerbread Granola Bars... 48

Quick and Easy Granola Bars 50

No-Bake Apple Sauce Granola Bars.. 52

No-Bake Choco Peanut Oatmeal Granola Bars 54

Honey Nut Granola 56

Granola Energy Bars 58

Honey Granola Breakfast Bars.. 60

No-Bake Cereal Bars... 62

Biography... 64

An Author's Afterthought 65

Introduction

Granola bars are healthy snacks to get you started on a good day. The typical granola bar is made of rolled oats (groats), nuts, sweetener, which is baked and cut into rectangles for your consumption. Today, granola bars contain everything from rice puffs, coconut, raisins, dates, and many vegan and healthy foods to their benefits in your body.

Granola bars can be baked to enhance the crunch and taste or left unbaked but stored well to prevent spoilage. Health-conscious people usually consume granola bars, but it is for everyone. Some health benefits of eating granola are:

- Lowers bad cholesterol

- Reduces the risk of chronic inflammation diseases

- Curbs hunger

Although granola is high in calories, it will provide your body with fiber, carbs, fats, and sugars needed when consumed accordingly. Do you have a granola bar recipe you love? If not, below are 30 recipes to get you started on a stress-free and healthy lifestyle?

OOOOOOOOOOOOOOOOOOOOOOOOOOOOOOOOOOOOOOOOO

No-Bake Flaked Coconut Granola Bars

These granola bars are quite different as in this recipe, marshmallows are used. The addition of flaked coconuts gives them a better taste.

Duration: 50 minutes

Serving Size: 36

List of Ingredients:

- Semi-sweet chocolate chips- 1 cup
- Butter- 1/3 cup
- Large marshmallows- 16
- Creamy peanut butter- 1/3 cup
- Vanilla extract- ½ tsp.
- Flaked coconut- 1 cup
- Rolled oats- 2 cups

OOOOOOOOOOOOOOOOOOOOOOOOOOOOOOOOOOOOOOOO

How to Cook:

Set a double boiler on a stove and melt the chocolate chips, butter, and marshmallows.

Mix until smooth and remove from heat.

Add the peanut butter, vanilla extract, flaked coconut, rolled oats, and mix everything properly.

Press the mixture into a greased baking tray and refrigerate for about 30 minutes or until they are set.

Serve!

Chewy Dry Fruit No-Bake Cookies

These chewy no-bake cookies taste amazing and are a must-try for everyone. The addition of dry fruits makes these cookies taste much better. You can use your favorite dry fruits to make these cookies.

Duration: 1 hour 15 minutes

Serving Size: 24

List of Ingredients:

- Oats- 1 cup
- Rolled oats- 1 cup
- Dry fruit- ½ cup
- Rice cereal- 1 cup
- Butter- ¼ cup
- Almonds- ½ cup
- Honey- ¼ cup
- Brown sugar- ½ cup
- Mini chocolate chips- ½ cup
- Vanilla extract- 2 tsp.

OOOOOOOOOOOOOOOOOOOOOOOOOOOOOOOOOOOOOOOOO

How to Cook:

Take a large bowl and add the oats, rice cereal, dry fruit, and chopped almonds together.

Mix these ingredients.

Take a saucepan, melt the butter (medium heat), and add the honey, brown sugar, and vanilla extract.

Mix it until the sugar is completely mixed.

Mix the oat mixture from another bowl in the butter mixture and mix.

Add the mixture to the baking dish and sprinkle over the mini chocolate chips.

Refrigerate for a few hours until it is chilled.

Cut into bars and serve!

No-Bake Fudgy Granola Bars

No baking is required in these granola bars. The cocoa powder gives a chocolaty taste to these bars.

Duration: 16 minutes.

Serving Size: 18

List of Ingredients:

- White sugar- 2 cups
- Milk- ½ cup
- Butter- ½ cup
- Peanut butter- ¾ cup
- Quick-cooking oats- 3 cups
- Cocoa powder- 6 tbsp.
- Vanilla extract- 1 tsp.
- Raisins- ½ cup

OOOOOOOOOOOOOOOOOOOOOOOOOOOOOOOOOOOOOOOOOO

How to Cook:

In a saucepan, add the white sugar, milk, and butter and bring it to a boil for at least 1 minute.

Remove the saucepan from heat and add the peanut butter, quick-cooking oats, cocoa powder, vanilla extract, and raisins. Mix well.

Press the mixture into a greased tray.

Let them rest and cool for 1 hour before serving.

Store in airtight containers.

No-Bake Oatmeal and Blueberry Bars

These granola bars taste well because of the addition of blueberries. The sweet flavor of the blueberries adds a lot of flavor to these bars.

Duration: 10 minutes

Serving Size: almost 20

List of Ingredients:

- White sugar- 2 cups
- Quick-cooking oats- 3 cups
- Blueberries- 1 cup
- Milk- ½ cup
- Margarine- ½ cup
- Vanilla extract- 1 tsp.

OOOOOOOOOOOOOOOOOOOOOOOOOOOOOOOOOOOOOOOOO

How to Cook:

In a saucepan, melt the margarine and add in the sugar.

Stir until dissolved.

Add the milk and stir until everything is mixed.

Remove from heat and cool.

Add in the vanilla extract, blueberries, and oats.

Put the mixture on a baking sheet and let them set.

Serve!

No-Bake Chocolate Granola Bars

These chocolate granola bars have a very friendly and unique flavor mainly because of the addition of chocolate. They are fairly quick and easy to make.

Duration: 10 minutes.

Serving Size: 24 to 30 bars.

List of Ingredients:

- Sugar- 2 cups
- Peanut butter- 3 tbsp.
- Vanilla extract- 1 tsp.
- Milk- ½ cup
- Quick oats- 3 cups
- Cocoa powder- ½ cup

OOOOOOOOOOOOOOOOOOOOOOOOOOOOOOOOOOOOOOOO

How to Cook:

In a pan over medium heat, add the sugar, cocoa powder, and milk and bring the mixture to a boil.

Let it boil for 3 minutes.

Remove it from heat, cool it. Add the vanilla extract, peanut butter, and quick oats and mix well.

Press the mixture into a tray, let them set before serving.

Flaked Coconut Granola Bars

This is a great recipe for coconut lovers and is a great chance to make these snowballs if you are planning a camping trip.

Duration: 20 minutes.

Serving Size: 24

List of Ingredients:

- Milk- 1 cup
- White sugar- 1 cup
- Butter- ¼ cup
- Unsweetened cocoa powder- ¼ cup
- Vanilla extract- 2 tsp.
- Rolled oats- 2 cups
- Shredded coconut- 2 ½ cups

OOOOOOOOOOOOOOOOOOOOOOOOOOOOOOOOOOOOOOOO

How to Cook:

In a pot, add the milk, white sugar, butter, and cocoa powder. Bring to boil for 3 minutes.

Now, add the vanilla extract and bring the mixture to boil for another 2 minutes.

Remove from heat and let it cool.

Now, add the oats and 2 cups of coconut to the milk mixture and mix it well. Cool it.

Press the mixture on a tray and sprinkle over the shredded coconut.

Let set before cutting and serving.

Gluten-Free and Oat-Free Granola Bars

An excellent way to avoid grains and sugars is with this recipe.

Duration: 10 minutes

Serving Size: 20

List of Ingredients:

- Almonds- 1 ¼ cups
- Sunflower seeds- 1 ¼ cups
- Shredded coconut- 2 cup
- Apricots- 1 cup
- Coconut oil- 1 ½ cups
- Honey- ½ cup
- Ground cinnamon- ¼ cup
- Vanilla extract- 1 tsp.
- Salt- ½ tsp.

OOOOOOOOOOOOOOOOOOOOOOOOOOOOOOOOOOOOOOOO

How to Cook:

Chop the almonds and the sunflower seeds into a food processor.

Now mix in the shredded coconut and the apricots, ground cinnamon, and salt.

In a saucepan, mix in the coconut oil, honey, and vanilla extract.

Pour this mixture into the coconut mixture and then mix.

Press this mixture into a tray and let set before cutting into bars and serving!

No-Bake Honey and Oat Peanut Granola Bars

These cookies are frozen and then eaten. These are perfect for the afternoon as a snack during teatime or else in kid's lunch boxes. These bars can also be of great help in camping and hiking trips.

Duration: 15 minutes

Serving Size: 16

List of Ingredients:

- Thick honey- 1/3 cup
- Chunky peanut butter- ¾ cup
- Vanilla extract- 1 tsp.
- Oatmeal- 1 cup
- Powdered milk- ¾ cup
- Sunflower seeds- ¼ cup
- Chocolate chips- ¼ cups

OOOOOOOOOOOOOOOOOOOOOOOOOOOOOOOOOOOOOOOO

How to Cook:

In a bowl, add in the thick honey and the peanut butter and mix.

Now add the vanilla extract, oatmeal, and powdered milk. Make sure that all the ingredients are mixed properly.

Add the sunflower seeds and mix.

Shape the mixture into balls and press to form a cookie shape or remain in their ball shapes.

Sprinkle with chocolate chips and freeze for 20 minutes before serving.

Chewy No-Bake Granola Bars

The addition of raisins in these bars gives them a very nice and unique flavor. It is a healthy recipe as raisins are quite good for our health. It is a great way to give these bars to kids because the flavor of chocolate will hide any taste of raisins in it.

Duration: 10 minutes

Serving Size: 36

List of Ingredients:

- Semisweet chocolate chips- 1 cup
- Light butter- 5 tbsp.
- Large marshmallows-14
- Vanilla extract- 1 tsp.
- Shredded raisins or any combination of the dry fruit mix, shredded coconut, miniature marshmallows or chopped nuts- 2/3 cup
- Uncooked quaker oats- 2 cups

OOOOOOOOOOOOOOOOOOOOOOOOOOOOOOOOOOOOOOOO

How to Cook:

Take a saucepan and add the semisweet chocolate chips, butter, and large marshmallows.

Heat them on low heat and stir until it turns into a smooth mixture.

Remove the saucepan from heat.

Cool slightly.

Now add in the vanilla extract.

Now add the quaker oats, shredded raisins, dry fruit mix, or shredded coconut (depending on your choice).

Mix properly so that all the ingredients are incorporated well.

Put the mixture into a greased tray and let it set before cutting.

Let them come at room temperature before serving to your guests.

Granola Bars with Oats

These granola bars can be made with a variety of flavors in the sense that instead of using this recipe, you can add in chocolate flavors or even blueberries.

Duration: 25 minutes

Serving Size: 48

List of Ingredients:

- White sugar- 2 cups
- Butter- ¾ cup
- Milk- 2/3 cup
- Quick-cooking oats- 3 ½ cups
- Vanilla extract- ½ tsp.

OOOOOOOOOOOOOOOOOOOOOOOOOOOOOOOOOOOOOOOO

How to Cook:

Take a pan, add in the sugar, butter, and milk, and bring it to a boil. Boil for 2 minutes.

Turn off the heat and cool slightly.

Add the oats and the vanilla extract.

Mix everything well, and then put it into a greased tray and let the bars set.

Serve!

Honey Peanut Granola

A lovely and crunchy homemade granola recipe with a mixture of ingredients.

Duration: 15 minutes

Serving Size:6

List of Ingredients:

- Oats- 3 cups
- Chopped peanuts- ½ cup
- Wheat germ- ¼ cup
- Honey- 1/3 cup
- Brown sugar- 1/3 cup
- Oil- ¼ cup
- Water- 2 tbsp.
- Salt- ½ tsp.
- Vanilla extract- 1 tsp.

OOOOOOOOOOOOOOOOOOOOOOOOOOOOOOOOOOOOOOOO

How to Cook:

Preheat your oven to 350 degrees Fahrenheit.

Mix the chopped peanuts, oats, and wheat germ.

Stir together the liquid mixture, the honey, brown sugar, oil, water, salt, and the vanilla extract, pour into the dry mix, and then mix.

Press the mixture into a greased baking tray and bake in a preheated oven for about an hour.

Cool before serving.

Snack Time Granola Bars

Make these fantastic granola bars for a perfect evening snack.

Duration: 10 minutes

Serving Size: 12

List of Ingredients:

- Flour- ¾ cup
- Wheat flour- ¾ cup
- Walnuts- ½ cup
- Salt- ¾ tsp.
- Baking powder- 2 tsp.
- Shortening- ½ cup
- Brown sugar- 1 ¾ cups
- Eggs- 2
- Vanilla extract- 1 tsp.
- Granola- 1 1/3 cups
- Cranberries- ½ cup

OOOOOOOOOOOOOOOOOOOOOOOOOOOOOOOOOOOOOOOO

How to Cook:

Preheat your oven to 350 degrees Fahrenheit.

Beat the shortening, brown sugar, eggs, and vanilla extract.

Cook the cranberries to soften them, chop, and then add to the egg mixture.

Now mix in the flour and wheat flour, salt, and baking powder.

Fold in the granola and mix properly.

Put the dough into a baking pan and bake in a preheated oven for 20 to 25 minutes.

Cool and cut into bars before serving them.

Chocolate Granola Bars

The amazing secret taste of these granola bars is because of the addition of chocolate drink mix powder instead of cocoa powder. The sweet chocolate drink mix gives an amazing taste to these granola bars.

Duration: 15 minutes.

Serving Size: 36

List of Ingredients:

- White sugar- 2 cups
- Salt- ½ tsp.
- Butter- ½ cup
- Milk- ½ cup
- Peanut butter- ½ cup
- Rolled oats- 3 cups
- Vanilla extract- 1 tsp.
- Powdered chocolate drink mix- ½ cup

OOOOOOOOOOOOOOOOOOOOOOOOOOOOOOOOOOOOOOOO

How to Cook:

Take a saucepan over medium heat and add the white sugar, salt, butter, and milk. Bring the mixture to boil and then boil for 1 minute.

Remove it from heat, cool it, and add the peanut butter, oats, vanilla extract, and powdered chocolate drink mix.

Press the mixture into a tray and let it set.

Let it rest and cool before serving.

Amazing Granola Snacks

A speedy and instant granola snack recipe which you would love to make every day.

Duration: 10 minutes

Serving Size:18

List of Ingredients:

- Crispy rice cereal- 2 ½ cups
- Oats- 2 cups
- Raisins- ½ cup
- Brown sugar- ½ cup
- Light corn syrup- ½ cup
- Peanut butter- ½ cup
- Vanilla extract- 1 tsp.

OOOOOOOOOOOOOOOOOOOOOOOOOOOOOOOOOOOOOOO

How to Cook:

Mix the crispy rice cereal, oats, and raisins.

Heat together the brown sugar and the corn syrup on low heat.

Remove from heat and mix in the peanut butter and the vanilla extract.

Mix in the oats mixture and mix well.

Pour into a prepared greased pan and let it cool before cutting and serving.

Vegan Coconut-Oat Bars

A straightforward recipe with lots of flavors.

Duration: 10 minutes

Serving Size: 8

List of Ingredients:

- Oats- 2 cups
- Bananas- 3
- Shredded coconut- ½ cup
- Chopped dates- ¼ cup
- Chopped walnuts- ¼ cup
- Honey- 3 tbsp.
- Vanilla extract- 1 tsp.
- Nutmeg- a pinch
- Salt- a pinch

OOOOOOOOOOOOOOOOOOOOOOOOOOOOOOOOOOOOOOO

How to Cook:

Preheat your oven to 350 degrees Fahrenheit.

Mix the oats, bananas, shredded coconut, chopped dates, walnuts, honey, vanilla extract, nutmeg, and salt.

Mix well and then press into a baking dish and bake in a preheated oven for 30 minutes.

Cut into bars and then serve!

Microwave Granola Bars

These granola bars are made in the microwave and are very easy and delicious.

Duration: 10 minutes

Serving Size: 8

List of Ingredients:

- Marshmallows- 1 cup
- Crispy rice cereal- 1 cup
- Oats- ¾ cup
- Honey- 2 tbsp.
- Butter- 1 tbsp.
- Chopped cranberries- ¼ cup
- Almonds- ¼ cup
- Ground cinnamon- a pinch

ooooooooooooooooooooooooooooooooooooooo

How to Cook:

Put the marshmallows into a microwave and melt for about 30 minutes.

Now mix in the crispy rice cereal, oats, honey, butter, chopped cranberries, almonds, and the ground cinnamon.

Press into a tray and then put in the freezer for 30 to 40 minutes until set.

Cut and serve!

Nut-Free Granola Bars

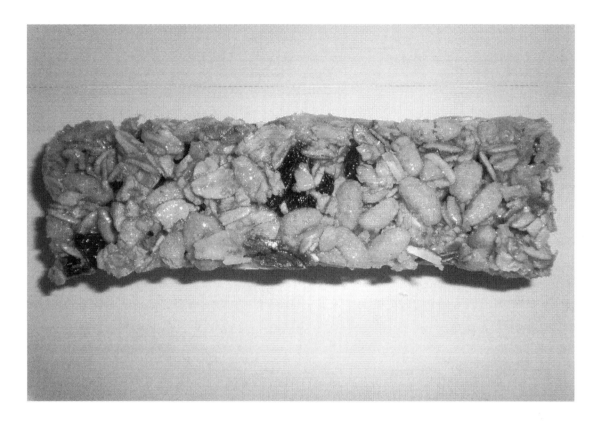

This is the perfect granola bar recipe for kids to give them in their lunch boxes.

Duration: 20 minutes

Serving Size: 16

List of Ingredients:

- Oats- 2 cups
- Flour- 1 cup
- Wheat germ- ½ cup
- Brown sugar- ¼ cup
- Chia seeds- 2 tbsp.
- Flax seeds- 2 tbsp.
- Cinnamon- 1 tsp.
- Salt- ½ tsp.
- Applesauce- 1 cup
- Honey- ½ cup
- Banana- 1
- Egg- 1
- Chopped dates- ¼ cup

OOOOOOOOOOOOOOOOOOOOOOOOOOOOOOOOOOOOOOOO

How to Cook:

Preheat your oven to 350 degrees Fahrenheit.

Mix the oats, flour, wheat germ, brown sugar, chia seeds, flax seeds, cinnamon, and salt.

In a blender, blend the applesauce, honey, banana, egg, and chopped dates.

Pour over the mixture into the oats mixture and mix well.

Put the mixture on a baking tray and bake in a preheated oven for 25 to 30 minutes.

Cool and cut into bars before serving.

No-Bake Chocolate Oat Bars

These no-bake chocolate oat bars are almost everyone's favorite and can be frozen for up to 10 days as well.

Duration: 30 minutes.

Serving Size: 32.

List of Ingredients:

- Butter-1 cup
- Peanut butter- ½ cup
- Brown sugar- ½ cup
- Vanilla extract- 1 tsp.
- Semisweet chocolate chips- 1 cup
- Quick-cooking oats- 3 cups

OOOOOOOOOOOOOOOOOOOOOOOOOOOOOOOOOOOOOOO

How to Cook:

Melt the butter in a saucepan and then add brown sugar, vanilla extract, and the quick-cooking oats.

Press them into a large dish.

Melt together the peanut butter and semisweet chocolate chips and pour it over the oats mixture.

Refrigerate for a good 3 hours before cutting it into bars and then serving it.

Simplest Granola Bars

These are easy to make with a lot of flexibility and great for hiking and road trips.

Duration: 5 minutes.

Serving Size:24.

List of Ingredients:

- Quick-cooking oats- 3 cups
- Condensed milk- 14 ounces
- Melted butter- 2 tbsp.
- Flaked coconut- 1 cup
- Sliced almonds- 1 cup
- Semisweet chocolate chips- 1 cup
- Dried cranberries- ½ cup

oooooooooooooooooooooooooooooooooooooooo

How to Cook:

Preheat your oven to 350 degrees Fahrenheit.

Mix the oats, condensed milk, melted butter, flaked coconut, sliced almonds, semisweet chocolate chips, and dried cranberries.

Press this mixture into a greased baking dish and put it to bake in the preheated oven for 20 to 25 minutes or until the edges become brown.

Cool, cut into bars, and then serve!

Healthy Nutella Granola Bars

An excellent addition of Nutella in this recipe makes it delicious.

Duration: 15 minutes

Serving Size: 24

List of Ingredients:

- Raisins- 1 cup
- Applesauce- ¾ cup
- Applesauce- 3 tbsp.
- Nutella- 2/3 cup
- Brown sugar- ½ cup
- Honey- ¼ cup
- Corn syrup- 2 tbsp.
- Vanilla extract- 2 tsp.
- Cinnamon- 1 tsp.
- Salt- 1 tsp.
- Oats- 3 1/3 cup
- Flour- 2/3 cup

OOOOOOOOOOOOOOOOOOOOOOOOOOOOOOOOOOOOOOOOOO

How to Cook:

Preheat your oven to 350 degrees Fahrenheit.

Mix the applesauce, Nutella, brown sugar, honey, corn syrup, vanilla extract, cinnamon, and salt.

Now mix in the oats and the flour and spread the mixture into a greased baking dish.

Put the dish to bake in preheated oven for 15 minutes.

Cut into bars and serve!

Gingerbread Granola Bars

The taste of ginger in these granola bars makes them taste delicious.

Duration: 15 minutes

Serving Size: 56

List of Ingredients:

- Oats- 8 cups
- Flour- 4 cups
- Brown sugar- 3 cups
- Sugar- ½ cup
- Salt- 1 tbsp.
- Cinnamon- 1 tbsp.
- Ground cloves- 1 ½ tsp.
- Ginger- 1 ½ tsp.
- Oil- 2 cups
- Honey- 1 cup
- Molasses- ¾ cup
- Eggs- 4
- Vanilla extract- 1 tbsp.

OOOOOOOOOOOOOOOOOOOOOOOOOOOOOOOOOOOOOOOOOO

How to Cook:

Preheat your oven to 350 degrees Fahrenheit.

Mix the oats, flour, brown sugar, salt, cinnamon, ground cloves, ginger, oil, honey, molasses, eggs, and vanilla extract.

Press the mixture into a greased baking tray and put the tray in a preheated oven to bake for 15 to 20 minutes.

Cool before cutting and serving.

Quick and Easy Granola Bars

A basic and simple granola bar recipe!

Duration: 15 minutes

Serving Size: 8

List of Ingredients:

- Oats- 2 cups
- Shredded coconut- ½ cup
- Honey- ½ cup
- Peanut butter- 2 tbsp.
- Vanilla extract- 1 tsp.
- Salt- 1/8 tsp.

OOOOOOOOOOOOOOOOOOOOOOOOOOOOOOOOOOOOOOOOO

How to Cook:

Preheat your oven to 325 degrees Fahrenheit.

Toast the oats and the coconut.

In a saucepan, mix the honey, peanut butter, salt, and vanilla extract.

Pour in the coconut and oat mixture and mix.

Press the mixture into a prepared baking dish and put it to bake for about 15 minutes.

Cool before cutting into bars and serving!

No-Bake Apple Sauce Granola Bars

These granola bars are very famous in America and a favorite of many. The addition of apple sauce gives these bars an interesting flavor.

Duration: 35 minutes

Serving Size: 40

List of Ingredients:

- White sugar- 1 2/3 cups
- Milk- ½ cup
- Cocoa powder- ½ cup
- Salt- 1/8 tsp.
- Peanut butter- ½ cup
- Applesauce- 5 tbsp.
- Vanilla extract- 1 tsp.
- Rolled oats- 3 cups

OOOOOOOOOOOOOOOOOOOOOOOOOOOOOOOOOOOOOOOOOO

How to Cook:

In a saucepan, add the milk, cocoa powder, and sugar, bring it to a boil, and cook it.

Move the saucepan from the stove and cool it slightly.

Add the peanut butter, apple sauce, salt, and vanilla extract and mix until completely smooth.

Now mix in the rolled oats.

Put the mixture into a greased baking tray and let it set before cutting and serving.

No-Bake Choco Peanut Oatmeal Granola Bars

This recipe is straightforward, and even the kids can help in making them. These are no-bake granola bars that do not need baking in the oven and can be made quickly.

Duration: 10 minutes.

Serving Size: 30

List of Ingredients:

- Milk- ½ cup
- White sugar- 2 cups
- Cocoa powder- 3 tbsp.
- Crunchy peanut butter- 3 tbsp.
- Butter- ½ cup
- Rolled oats- 3 cups
- Vanilla extract- 1 tsp.

OOOOOOOOOOOOOOOOOOOOOOOOOOOOOOOOOOOOOOOOO

How to Cook:

In a saucepan, add the milk, white sugar, cocoa powder, butter, and peanut butter and bring them to boil over medium heat.

Boil for 1.30 minutes and do not stir.

Remove the saucepan from heat and let it cool.

Now add the rolled oats and the vanilla extract.

Stir the mixture until the oats are distributed fairly.

Put the mixture in on a greased tray.

Let them cool before serving.

You can store it in airtight containers.

Honey Nut Granola

A very delicious and crunchy breakfast treat!

Duration: 10 minutes

Serving Size:20

List of Ingredients:

- Oats- 4 cups
- Almonds- 1 cup
- Chopped pecans- 1 cup
- Sunflower seeds- 1 cup
- Oil- 1/3 cup
- Honey- ½ cup
- Vanilla extract- 1 tsp.
- Cinnamon- 1 tbsp.

OOOOOOOOOOOOOOOOOOOOOOOOOOOOOOOOOOOOOOOO

How to Cook:

Preheat your oven to 300 degrees Fahrenheit.

Mix the oats, almonds, chopped pecans, sunflower seeds, oil, honey, vanilla extract, and cinnamon.

Press the mixture into a prepared baking tray.

Put the tray to bake in preheated oven for 10 minutes.

Cut and then serve!

Granola Energy Bars

These energy bars can be made just with the three ingredients and are incredibly healthy and great for camping trips.

Duration: 10 minutes

Serving Size: 16

List of Ingredients:

- Nuts- 1 cup
- Dried fruit- 1 cup
- Dried dates- 12 to 15

OOOOOOOOOOOOOOOOOOOOOOOOOOOOOOOOOOOOOOOOOO

How to Cook:

Roast the nuts to brown them in a preheated oven at 350 degrees Fahrenheit.

Remove the seeds from the dates.

Take a food processor and add in the nuts, dates, and dried fruit, and mix.

Form balls from the mixture and then shape them into square shapes and place them on the tray.

Refrigerate the squares for an hour.

Serve!

Honey Granola Breakfast Bars

A healthy mix of oats, nuts, dried fruit, and honey makes it a perfect breakfast.

Duration: 20 minutes

Serving Size: 12

List of Ingredients:

- Oats- 2 cups
- Chopped walnuts- 1 cup
- Brown sugar- ¾ cup
- Dried fruit- ¾ cup
- Flour- ½ cup
- Wheat flour- ½ cup
- Wheat germ- ½ cup
- Ground cinnamon- ¾ tsp.
- Salt- ¾ tsp.
- Oil- ½ cup
- Honey- ½ cup
- Egg- 1
- Vanilla extract- 2 tsp.

OOOOOOOOOOOOOOOOOOOOOOOOOOOOOOOOOOOOOOOO

How to Cook:

Preheat your oven to 350 degrees Fahrenheit.

Mix the oats, chopped walnuts, brown sugar, dried fruit, flour, wheat flour, wheat germ, ground cinnamon, and salt.

In another bowl, mix the oil, honey, egg, and vanilla extract.

Pour over the dry mixture and press the mixture into a baking tray.

Put the tray to bake in preheated oven for 20 to 25 minutes.

Cut when cool and serve!

No-Bake Cereal Bars

These cereal bars are easy and quick to make. They taste wonderful.

Duration: 10 minutes.

Serving Size: 36

List of Ingredients:

- Brown sugar- ½ cup
- Light corn syrup- 1/3 cup
- Vanilla extract- 1 tsp.
- Peanut butter- 3/4th cup
- Flake cereal- 3 cups
- Coconut- 1 cup

OOOOOOOOOOOOOOOOOOOOOOOOOOOOOOOOOOOOOOOOOOO

How to Cook:

Take a pan, add the brown sugar and the light corn syrup, and bring it to a boil.

When it starts to boil, add the vanilla extract and the peanut butter and stir it well.

Remove from heat and add the flake cereal and the coconut.

Spray the cookie sheet with a nonstick cooking spray and press the mixture on the cookie sheet.

Let them cool before serving.

Biography

For decades, this beautiful actress graced our screens with her incredible talent and performance in movies that captivated the script and emotions of the viewers. Well, life rarely goes as planned, but we should always make the best out of it, like Chloe.

Originally from the bubbly city of Los Angeles, she has moved from the movie industry into the food scene. Her role in Mama Mia ignited her passion for food. She has taken the New York scene by surprise. Charmed by the unique regions she had visited, the delicious delicacies she tasted, her uncanny appreciation for flavors, ingredients, and cooking techniques have continued to wow customers wide and far.

However, as mentioned, she started as an actress. Breaking into the food scene was easy because she had contacts and connections, but satisfying clients was a different ball game. Over the years, she has mastered the food scenes and unique flavors clients seek. Today, her clients can attest to the high-quality food from her restaurants.

The New York food scene is a jungle that only the strong dare to tread. However, she was a passionate student and learned the tricks and tips, and slowly set her passion for delivering excellent tastes to all who sought them.

An Author's Afterthought

Did you like my book? I pondered it severely before releasing this book. Although the response has been overwhelming, it is always pleasing to see, read or hear a new comment. Thank you for reading this and I would love to hear your honest opinion about it. Furthermore, many people are searching for a unique book, and your feedback will help me gather the right books for my reading audience.

Thanks!

Chloe Tucker

Printed in Great Britain
by Amazon

83023827R00038